World Book's Documenting History
World War II in Europe

WORLD BOOK

a Scott Fetzer company
Chicago

www.worldbook.com

World Book, Inc.
233 N. Michigan Avenue
Chicago, IL 60601
U.S.A.

For information about other World Book publications, visit our website at **http://www.worldbook.com**
or call **1-800-WORLDBK (967-5325).**

For information about sales to schools and libraries, call **1-800-975-3250 (United States)**, or **1-800-837-5365 (Canada).**

Library of Congress Cataloging-in-Publication Data

World War II in Europe.
    p. cm. -- (World Book's documenting history)
    Summary: "A history of World War II as it was fought in Europe, based on primary source documents and other historical artifacts. Features include period art works and photographs; excerpts from literary works, letters, speeches, broadcasts, and diaries; summary boxes; a timeline; maps; and a list of additional resources"-- Provided by publisher.
    Includes bibliographical references and index.
    ISBN 978-0-7166-1509-5
    1. World War, 1939-1945--Europe--Juvenile literature. 2. World War, 1939-1945--Europe--Sources--Juvenile literature. I. World Book, Inc. II. Title: World War 2 in Europe. III. Title: World War Two in Europe.
    D756.W67 2011
    940.54'21--dc22
                                        2010008911

World Book's Documenting History
Set ISBN 978-0-7166-1498-2 (hc.)

Also available as:
ISBN: 978-0-7166-1667-2 (pbk.)

Printed by Book Partners
A division of The HF Group
North Manchester, Indiana

Contents

The Background to War

BEFORE WORLD WAR I (1914-1918), GERMANY WAS ONE OF THE MOST powerful countries in Europe. The *unification* (joining into one) of the German states into the country of Germany in 1871 had created a powerful and proud new nation in the middle of Europe. But, in 1918, Germany lost World War I, along with more than 2 million of its citizens. The victors of the war, the Allied nations—which included France, the United Kingdom, and the United States—required Germany to pay war damages and give up territory. Many Germans felt the war could have been won and blamed their defeat on the government—and rich bankers and industrialists.

In the early 1920's, Germany's fragile economy collapsed as *inflation* (a continual increase in prices throughout a nation's economy) destroyed the value of money. The economy slowly recovered, only to be crushed by the Great Depression, a worldwide economic crisis that began in 1929. Millions of Germans lost their jobs, leading to social unrest and violence.

◀ A detail of a painting by Irish artist Sir William Orpen (1878-1931) shows the signing of the 1919 Treaty of Versailles, which officially ended World War I. The German delegation faces U.S. President Woodrow Wilson (1856-1924), shown holding a document, with French Premier Georges Clemenceau (1841-1929) on Wilson's left and British Prime Minister David Lloyd George (1863-1945), on Wilson's right. Many Germans felt humiliated by the terms of the treaty.

▶ The Treaty of Versailles was signed on June 28, 1919. It forced Germany to accept all of the blame for the war; to give up its colonies and some European territory; and to shrink its army to the point where the nation was nearly defenseless. It also required Germany to pay the Allied nations enormous *reparations* (payments for war damages).

Article 119: Germany *renounces* [gives up] . . . all her rights and titles over her *overseas possessions* [colonies].

Article 160: The German army must not *comprise* [be made up of] more than seven divisions of *infantry* [foot soldiers] and three divisions of *cavalry* [troops on horseback].

Articles 231 and 233: Germany accepts the responsibility . . . for causing all the loss and damage . . . as a consequence of the war . . . for which *compensation* [payment] is to be made by Germany.

excerpts from the Treaty of Versailles

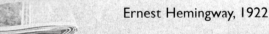

▲ Germans living abroad protesting the Treaty of Versailles. The banners read, "We foreign Germans protest against the forced peace and against the robbery of our private property."

▶ In the Sept. 19, 1922, *Toronto Star,* American author Ernest Hemingway (1899-1961) describes Germany after World War I. Hemingway witnessed firsthand the effects of runaway inflation in Germany. People from France would cross into Kehl, a German town on the French border, to buy German goods with French currency. German paper money had become all but worthless a few years after the war. In 1919, $1 in U.S. currency was worth a little more than 8 German marks. By 1923, $1 in U.S. currency was worth over 4 trillion marks.

We changed some French money in the railway station at Kehl. For ten francs I received 670 [German] marks. Ten francs amounted to about ninety cents in Canadian money . . . the French cannot come over to Kehl and buy up all the cheap goods they would like to. But they can come over and eat. It is a sight every afternoon to see the mob that storms the German pastry shops and tea places . . . . [a] *proprietor* [owner] and his helper were *surly* [bad-tempered] and didn't seem particularly happy when all the cakes were sold. The mark was falling faster than they could bake.

Ernest Hemingway, 1922

NOW YOU KNOW

- Germany was defeated in World War I, but many Germans felt they could have won the war.
- The 1919 Treaty of Versailles humiliated Germany and required Germany to pay a huge amount of reparations, weakening the economy.
- Runaway inflation destroyed the Germany economy in the early 1920's.

The Rise of the Nazis

THE GREAT DEPRESSION LEFT MILLIONS OF GERMANS UNEMPLOYED and desperate. Many working-class people turned to the Communist and Socialist parties. Others supported *right wing* (extremely conservative) groups like the Nazi Party, led by Adolf Hitler (1889-1945). The Nazis promised to improve the economy, overturn the Treaty of Versailles, and rebuild Germany's military power. Hitler blamed Communists, Jews, and others for Germany's defeat in the war and the hard times that followed. Although many people did not take him seriously, Hitler's magnetic speeches won him many followers. After gaining political control of Germany in 1933, Hitler won the support of many businessmen by crushing liberal parties and labor unions. He promised to build a mighty empire that would last 1,000 years.

◀ Nazi storm troopers—a private army created by Adolf Hitler—march as part of the 1938 Nuremberg Rally. The Nazi Party staged rallies in Nuremberg annually from 1923 through 1938. As Adolf Hitler gained control of Germany in 1933, the state used the rallies as *propaganda events* (events giving one-sided information meant to influence opinion) to emphasize the bond between the people and the Nazi Party.

2

Suddenly the beat of the drums increased and three motor-cycles with yellow standards [flags] fluttering from their windshields raced through the gates. A few minutes later a fleet of black cars rolled swiftly into the arena: in one of them, standing in the front seat, his hand outstretched in the Nazi salute, was Hitler. . . . Some of the audience began swaying back and forth, chanting Sieg Heil ["Hail Victory"] over and over again in a frenzy [great excitement] of delirium [madness]. I looked at the faces around me and saw tears streaming down people's cheeks. The drums had grown louder and I suddenly felt frightened.

an eyewitness to the
1938 Nuremberg Rally

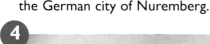 An eyewitness describes the 1938 Nazi rally in the German city of Nuremberg.

4

Naturally, I myself am extremely cautious, since I am in a particularly dangerous position and have to think of my wife and children. When teaching my class, I am not merely 100 per cent Nazi, I am 150 per cent.

a German schoolteacher, 1940

3

▲ Members of Hitler Youth participate in a "human chariot race" at a summer camp in the mid-1930's. Hitler Youth for boys emphasized physical and military training. It was designed to fill young men with Nazi ideals and motivate them to become good German soldiers. After 1939, all German boys and girls between the ages of 10 and 18 were required to join Hitler Youth.

◀ A schoolteacher expresses the fear that kept many people from rebelling when Hitler threw the country into what would become World War II and mass destruction. The teacher's writing was published in *Uncensored Germany*, a book of letters collected by a German political party that opposed Hitler. This anti-Nazi propaganda was printed by a British publisher in 1940.

NOW YOU KNOW

- Hitler blamed Communists and Jews for Germany's problems.
- Hitler gained political control of Germany in 1933.
- The Nazi Party worked to attract young people to their cause and used fear to silence *dissent* (disagreement) and stop rebellion.

The Road to War

GERMANY BEGAN TO FORM AN *ALLIANCE* (UNION FORMED BY AGREEMENT) with Benito Mussolini (1883-1945), the dictator of Italy, in 1936. Most other European governments did not support the Nazis, but they did not interfere when Germany took over Austria in March 1938. Hitler then turned his sights on Czechoslovakia. Nearly 3 million people who were German-speaking lived in a part of Czechoslovakia called the Sudetenland. Hitler demanded that the Sudetenland also become part of Germany. In September 1938, France and the United Kingdom agreed to Hitler's demand in a pact called the Munich Agreement. Both nations hoped that the agreement would prevent—or at least delay—war. This policy of trying to satisfy Hitler to prevent war, or at least prolong peace to prepare for war, proved unsuccessful.

1

German-Austria must return to the great German mother country. . . . One blood demands one *Reich* [empire or state].

Mein Kampf,
Adolf Hitler

◀ Hitler describes his belief that Austria is a natural part of Germany in his book *Mein Kampf* (*My Struggle*), published in two parts in 1925 and 1926. The book is part autobiography and part political theory. In it, Hitler also makes his thoughts about the Soviet Union and Europe's Jews very clear: he describes Communists and Jews as the world's twin evils.

▶ Austrians greet German soldiers as they enter Vienna, the capital of Austria, in 1938. The Treaty of Versailles carved up the Austro-Hungarian Empire into new states that included Austria and Hungary. The new country of Czechoslovakia was also created from the old empire. Hitler, an Austrian by birth, claimed that German-speaking Austria was a natural part of Germany. In March 1938, he forced a union between the two countries, and the German Army marched into Austria, welcomed by cheering crowds. Austria became a province of Germany. Hitler had rejected the terms of the Treaty of Versailles, and no one had tried to stop him.

2

3

▶ British Prime Minister Neville Chamberlain (1869-1940) waves the Munich Agreement in triumph to a crowd in London. In the agreement, dated Sept. 29, 1938, Czechoslovakia surrendered the Sudetenland, a German-speaking border area, to Germany. In return, Hitler pledged a halt to German aggression.

4

We, the German *Führer* [Hitler's title] . . . and the British Prime Minister . . . regard the agreement signed last night [the Munich Agreement] and the Anglo-German Naval Agreement as *symbolic of* [standing for] the desire of our two peoples never to go to war with one another again.

from the Anglo-German Declaration, 1938

▲ The Anglo-German Declaration—a pledge of peace between Nazi Germany and the United Kingdom—was signed on Sept. 30, 1938, shortly after the signing of the Munich Agreement.

▶ A speech broadcast on radio in which Neville Chamberlain discusses the declaration after his return from Munich. Chamberlain uses the phrase, "peace for our time." This became one of history's great *ironic statements*—meaning it was very contrary to the events that occurred; six months later Hitler seized the rest of Czechoslovakia.

5

I believe it is peace for our time. We thank you from the bottom of our hearts. And now I recommend you to go home and sleep quietly in your beds.

Neville Chamberlain, 1938

NOW YOU KNOW

- Nazi Germany marched into Austria in March 1938.
- The British accepted the Nazi takeover of the Sudetenland of Czechoslovakia.
- The Munich Agreement was meant to stop Nazi aggression, but it did not.

The Invasion of Poland

IN THE TREATY OF VERSAILLES, GERMANY *CEDED* (HANDED OVER) German territory in the east to Poland. As Germany began to rebuild its military after Hitler's rise to power, many feared it would try to retake the territory lost to Poland. France and the United Kingdom promised to protect Poland, but Adolf Hitler did not think they would go to war to do so. Hitler felt especially safe because he had signed a treaty with Joseph Stalin (1879-1953), the dictator of the Soviet Union. In the public part of the treaty, Hitler and Stalin agreed not to war against each other. In a secret part of the treaty, they agreed to carry out a joint invasion and *occupation* (sending soldiers to hold possession) of Poland.

On Sept. 1, 1939, Germany invaded Poland. Two days later, France and the United Kingdom declared war on Germany. World War II had begun. On September 17, the Soviet Union invaded Poland from the east.

> ... The destruction of Poland has priority [the most importance]. ... I shall give a propagandist reason for starting the war, no matter whether it is plausible [believable] or not. The victor will not be asked afterwards whether he told the truth or not.

Adolf Hitler before the invasion of Poland

> The Germans in Poland are being persecuted [treated cruelly and unfairly] by bloody terror and are being driven from their homesteads [homes and lands]. ... To put an end to this lunacy, there remains no other recourse for me but to meet force with force.

Adolf Hitler upon the invasion of Poland

▲ German troops cross the border into Poland in September 1939. German and Soviet forces defeated the Polish Army after five weeks of combat. More than 60,000 Polish troops were killed, along with many thousands of civilians.

▶ The first quote is from Hitler's declaration to his army commanders on Aug. 22, 1939. The second quote is the "propagandist reason" Hitler invented to justify invading Poland. Hitler stated this to his troops on Sept. 1, 1939.

3

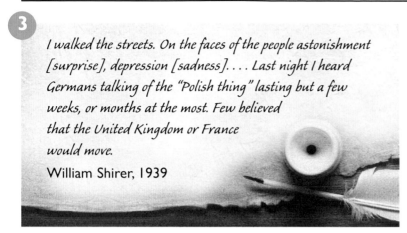

I walked the streets. On the faces of the people astonishment [surprise], depression [sadness]. . . . Last night I heard Germans talking of the "Polish thing" lasting but a few weeks, or months at the most. Few believed that the United Kingdom or France would move.

William Shirer, 1939

◀ In *Berlin Diary* (1941), the published version of a journal kept by U.S. reporter and historian William Shirer (1904-1993), the author describes the surprised mood in Germany's capital when war was declared by the United Kingdom and France on Sept. 3, 1939. Shirer was living in Europe as a foreign reporter for Columbia Broadcasting System (CBS) radio.

4

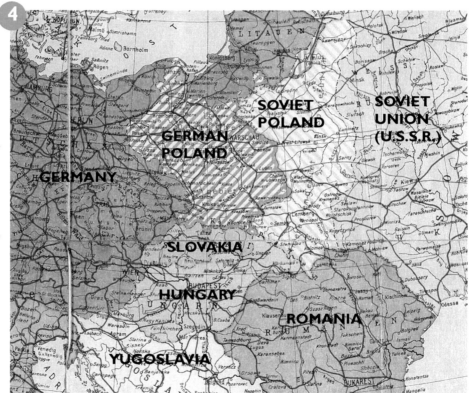

▶ A 1939 map of Europe. After being invaded from both sides, Poland was divided between Germany and the Soviet Union. The Nazis now controlled the lives of more than 2 million Polish Jews, people they considered to be an inferior race.

NOW YOU KNOW

- Nazi Germany invaded Poland on Sept. 1, 1939, triggering World War II in Europe.

- Two days later, France and the United Kingdom declared war on Germany.

- The Soviet Union invaded Poland on Sept. 17, 1939. Germany and the Soviet Union divided Poland's territory between them.

Early Nazi Conquests

Following World War I, France built a string of concrete forts and defenses along the German border. The defenses—called the Maginot Line—were meant to stop a German invasion. In May 1940, however, German troops went around the Maginot Line, invading France through Belgium and the Netherlands. France fell within six weeks. Germany had already invaded Denmark and Norway in April. With the occupation of France, Belgium, and the Netherlands, much of Europe was under German rule by June.

Just before France's surrender, on June 10, 1940, Italian dictator Benito Mussolini declared war on France and the United Kingdom. In September 1940, Germany, Italy, and Japan formed an alliance known as the Axis powers. The Axis powers were opposed by the Allies—France, the United Kingdom, and eventually the Soviet Union, United States, and many other nations.

▶ In a journal entry, German Field Marshal Erwin Rommel (1891-1944), who led a successful invasion force into France in 1940, remembers the frustration German soldiers had felt fighting World War I.

We were through the Maginot Line! . . . Twenty-two years before we had stood for four and a half years before this self-same enemy and had won victory after victory and yet finally lost the war. And now we had broken though [famous] Maginot Line and were driving deep into enemy territory.

Erwin Rommel, 1940

◀ Allied troops at Dunkirk in 1940. With the collapse of France, a large force of British and other Allied soldiers withdrew to the French port of Dunkirk. More than 300,000 troops were safely taken from Dunkirk to England in late May and early June of 1940. In addition to naval ships, private ferries, fishing boats, and pleasure boats were used to evacuate the Allied forces.

3

I observed his [Hitler's] face. It was grave, solemn [serious], yet brimming with revenge. There was also in it, as in his springy step, a note of the triumphant conqueror, the defier [one who refuses to obey] of the world. There was something else, difficult to describe, in his expression, a sort of scornful [lacking respect], inner joy at being present at this great reversal of fate—a reversal he himself had wrought [made]...

William Shirer, 1940

▲ American journalist William Shirer describes the French surrender to Germany in 1940 in a diary entry. Still angered by Germany's defeat in World War I, Adolf Hitler took great pride in Germany's quick victories at the beginning of World War II. Hitler was especially pleased with the surrender of France.

▶ Adolf Hitler (in the front row, second from the right) marches proudly with Nazi officers before the Eiffel Tower in Paris. Such images greatly influenced German public opinion.

4

NOW YOU KNOW

- Germany invaded and defeated France and several other countries in western Europe in 1940.
- More than 300,000 British and other Allied troops were rescued at the port of Dunkirk.
- The German conquest of France was seen by many as an act of revenge for Germany's defeat in World War I.

Germany Attacks Britain

WHEN THE UNITED KINGDOM REFUSED TO FORM A PACT with the Nazis, Hitler planned to invade the island nation. His first task was to destroy the British Royal Air Force (RAF). German warplanes began the air assault—known as the Battle of Britain—on July 10, 1940. The battle began against RAF targets, such as airfields and aircraft factories. The RAF survived the attacks, and the Germans shifted their attention to the bombing of British cities. The bombing attacks—called the Blitz—began in September of 1940 and continued through May 1941. The word *Blitz* came from the German word *Blitzkrieg* (lightning war). The bravery of the RAF during the Battle of Britain prompted a famous tribute from the British prime minister, Winston Churchill (1874-1965): "Never in the field of human conflict was so much owed by so many to so few."

Hitler had wanted to defeat the United Kingdom before launching an attack against the Soviet Union, but British resistance continued. Germany decided this resistance was not a threat to their hold on Europe, and in early summer of 1941 the Germans moved their armies to the Soviet border.

▶ A London street after Nazi Germany's air force, the *Luftwaffe* (German for *air weapon*), launched the Blitz in 1940. While the Germans bombed many British cities, the Blitz began with the bombing of London for 57 straight days and nights.

2

On the way into town, two women at the bus stop here: "Heil [Hail] Hitler!"— "What have you heard from your boy?"— "Good news a week ago, they're looking forward to England."... Then at the butcher: "It's just been on the wireless: 'The English government has fallen.' Now there'll be peace. Very good, why should they let themselves be shot to pieces first?"
Berlin rumors, 1940

THE ILLUSTRATED LONDON NEWS

The World Copyright of all the Editorial Matter, both Illustrations and Letterpress, is Strictly Reserved in Great Britain, the British Dominions and Colonies, Europe, and the United States of America

SATURDAY, SEPTEMBER 14, 1940.

◀ A Berlin professor, Victor Klemperer (1881-1960), recorded in his diary what he heard on the streets on July 7, 1940, including the false rumor that the British government had fallen. The professor's diaries for 1933-1941 were published in English in the 1990's as *I Will Bear Witness*.

▲ A German Messerschmitt fighter over the south coast of England in October 1940. During 1940 and 1941, German warplanes became a familiar sight in the skies over England. The Nazis raided British towns and ports—killing more than 40,000 people—but they failed to destroy the RAF.

▶ British pilot John Beard, in an interview published in *Their Finest Hour* (1941), describes a brief encounter with two enemy fighters during the Battle of Britain in September 1940. The Battle of Britain was launched by Nazi Germany in July 1940 and continued through October.

At that moment some instinct made me glance up at my rear-view mirror and spot two Messerschmitts [German planes] were closing in on my tail. Instantly I hauled back on the [joy] stick and streaked upward. And just in time. For as I flicked into the climb, I saw the *tracer streaks* [trails from bullets fired from the enemy plane] pass beneath me. As I turned, I had a quick look round the "office" [cockpit]. My fuel reserve was running out and I had only about a second's supply of ammunition left. I was certainly in no condition to take on two Messerschmitts. But they seemed no more eager than I was. Perhaps they were in the same position, for they turned away for home. I put my nose down and did likewise.

British pilot describes the Battle of Britain

NOW YOU KNOW

- Hitler planned an invasion of the United Kingdom.
- The Germans failed to destroy the RAF during the Battle of Britain.
- British cities were heavily bombed in what became known as the Blitz.

The Sorrow of the Jews

BEFORE COMING TO POWER IN 1933, HITLER BLAMED JEWS for many of Germany's problems. After 1933, a series of laws was ordered that *isolated* (kept apart) Jews from the social and cultural life of Germany. Jews were forbidden to work as teachers, lawyers, or physicians. Books by Jewish writers were burned in public. German Jews eventually lost their citizenship and were forbidden to marry non-Jews. Further laws made it illegal for Jews to own or run a business or to go to a cinema or public bath.

▶ In *Forgotten Voices of the Holocaust* (2005), Christabel Bielenberg, interviewed after the war, remembers what her Jewish doctor told her in the late 1930's in Hamburg, Germany. In Nazi Germany, the word "Aryan" would have meant a person who was not Jewish; thus, the physician was forbidden to treat the children of Christians.

▼ Ruins of a Jewish-owned shop in Berlin. On November 9-10, 1938, synagogues, shops, and homes of Jewish people were attacked and burned. There was so much broken glass after the attacks that the destruction became known as *Kristallnacht* (German for "crystal night," meaning "night of the broken glass"). Thousands of Jews were arrested and sent to concentration camps—special prisons for supposed enemies of the Nazi state.

1

"I would like to tell you, Mrs. Bielenberg, that I can't look after your child any more, you'll have to take a new doctor." That, I remember, was the first huge shock. I said, "A new doctor, for goodness sake why?" And he said, "As you know, I was head of the clinic here in which I invested a lot of my earnings. I have been banned from that; it's been taken away from me and I have had a letter which said that I am not allowed to lay my hands on 'Aryan' children ever again."

a woman describes life in
Nazi Germany in the late 1930's

2

3

4

▲ The yellow star the Jewish people were ordered to wear by the Nazis made them a target for attacks.

▲ Jewish children beg in the streets of the ghetto in Poland's capital, Warsaw, in 1941. In Poland, the Nazis openly mistreated and murdered Jews. Special killing squads were created to select Polish Jews for execution. Those not murdered were ordered after 1940 to live within special walled areas in cities, called *ghettos*, and their food was restricted. Thousands died from starvation and disease. In 1942, hundreds of thousands of the people trapped in the Warsaw ghetto were sent to death camps.

▶ A German police order of Sept. 1, 1941, declares that Jews must identify themselves in public in Nazi Germany.

5

1. Jews above the age of six are forbidden to show themselves in public without the Jews' star.

2. The Jews' star consists of a black-edged, six-pointed star of yellow cloth, as large as the palm of the hand, with the word *JUDE* [German for "Jew"] in black. It must be clearly visible, firmly sewn to the left breast of the piece of clothing.

German police order

NOW YOU KNOW

- Hitler introduced laws to isolate Jews from German society.
- *Kristallnacht* was a night of violent attacks on German Jews.
- In Poland, Jews were murdered or forced into ghettos.

The War Spreads

IN SEPTEMBER 1940, ITALIAN TROOPS INVADED EGYPT, THREATENING THE BRITISH forces that were protecting the Suez Canal. Italy also invaded Albania and Greece, bringing the war to southeastern Europe. The United States became more involved in supporting the Allies. American *merchant* (nonmilitary) ships aided British merchant ships, carrying badly needed supplies across the Atlantic Ocean to the United Kingdom. Without these supplies, the British might not have been able to continue in the war. German *U-boats* (submarines) attacked the merchant ships to prevent materials from reaching the Allies. The merchant ships traveled in *convoys* (groups of ships) protected by warships and warplanes to defend against U-boat attacks. This struggle for control of the Atlantic Ocean, known as the Battle of the Atlantic, ran from 1939 to 1945 and took the lives of around 30,000 Allied merchant sailors.

1 ◀ A German postcard with a poem praises a famous German submarine commander—and the sinking of an Allied warship. U-boats enjoyed much early success, but the tide eventually turned against them. Technological advances, such as new weapons, *sonar* (a system that uses sound energy to locate objects), and improvements in *radar* (an electronic instrument used to locate objects) made it more difficult for the U-boats. Around 28,000 German submariners died in the war— about two out of every three in the service.

2 Everyone aboard looked alike, smelled alike, had adopted the same phrases and curses. We had learned to live together in a narrow tube no longer than two railroad cars. We . . . became experts on each others habits. . . . The pressure mounted with the passage of each uneventful day, but it could be relieved in an instant by the sight of a fat convoy.

Herbert A. Werner

▶ Herbert A. Werner (1920-   ), commander of a German U-boat, describes life on board a U-230 in his book *Iron Coffins* (1969).

▲ German *panzers* (armored vehicles, or tanks) in North Africa. In February 1941, Adolf Hitler sent German troops to support the Italians in Africa, where fighting began in June 1940. Forces from Australia, Canada, India, New Zealand, and the United States joined the British in fighting the Axis powers in this region. The war in the desert raged until 1943, when forces under German Field Marshal Erwin Rommel were forced to withdraw.

▶ In a journal entry from October 1942, Field Marshal Erwin Rommel describes the difficulty he faces with the war in Africa. Rommel was known as the Desert Fox because of his clever strategies in the African campaign.

Only 70 tons of petrol [gasoline] had been flown across by the Luftwaffe [German Air Force] that day with the result that the army could only refuel for a short distance, for there was no knowing when petrol would arrive in any quantity and how long the divisions would have to get along with the few tons we could issue to them.

Erwin Rommel, 1942

NOW YOU KNOW

- The war in Europe spread to North Africa and southeastern Europe.
- The United States supported the Allies with supplies of badly needed materials.
- German submarines, called U-boats, attacked Allied merchant ships in the Atlantic Ocean.

The Invasion of the U.S.S.R.

AFTER QUICK VICTORIES IN POLAND, SCANDINAVIA, AND WESTERN EUROPE, Hitler's armies invaded the Soviet Union in June 1941. The attack came as a surprise to the Soviet dictator Joseph Stalin, though his secret agents had warned of the coming invasion. Stalin had trusted in the treaty he had signed with Hitler (see page 10). Despite the huge size of the Soviet Red Army, Hitler was confident of victory. At first, the German Army—supported by its allies—drove the Red Army back. By December, hundreds of thousands of Soviet soldiers had been killed and more than 3 million others had been captured, while the Germans had lost 200,000 soldiers. Ordinary people caught in the fire storm of this invasion suffered terribly—especially the Jews. More than 1 million Jews died in the Soviet Union before the war's end.

▶ A Soviet poster reads "Beat the German beasts, you can and must *exterminate* (destroy) Hitler's army." The Soviet Union was unprepared for the German invasion—more than 3 million German troops and some 600,000 troops of German allies swarmed the Soviet Union, beginning on June 22, 1941. The Soviets lost incredible numbers of people and huge amounts of equipment and territory in the first months of fighting. But Soviet resistance stiffened and had reorganized by August. Millions of fresh Soviet troops were rushed to the front, while entire factories were taken apart and moved eastward to be rebuilt out of reach of the Germans. Then the brutal Soviet winter set in.

БЕЙ НЕМЕЦКИХ ЗВЕРЕЙ!
УНИЧТОЖИТЬ ГИТЛЕРОВСКУЮ АРМИЮ—МОЖНО И ДОЛЖНО.

2

The Soviets also proved exceptionally adept at preparing towns and villages for defense, converting them into virtual *fortresses* [forts] very quickly. Wooden houses sported well-camouflaged gun ports almost flush with the floor, their interiors reinforced with dirt or sandbags, and observation slots cut into the roofs. *Bunkers* [underground shelters] were excavated into the floors connected with adjacent houses or exterior defenses by narrow trenches. Although almost all inhabited places were crammed with Red Army troops, they appeared deserted to German *reconnaissance* [initial inspection mission] units, since even water and food details were allowed to leave their shelters only after dark.

German General Erhard Raus

▲ German General Erhard Raus (1889-1956) explains the difficulty German soldiers had in identifying enemy positions during the invasion of the Soviet Union, in a work published after the war.

3

According to the military bulletins, tremendous success in the East, one million prisoners etc., battle at Smolensk—nothing but annihilation [destruction] of the Russians. According to what one hears otherwise . . . Germany's position most precarious [dangerous], total victory over Russia before onset of winter impossible, lasting through the winter next to impossible, given shortages of raw materials. Who is right?

Berlin professor, 1941

▶ Berlin professor Victor Klemperer describes conflicting reports about the course of the war in his diary in August 1941. The official government reports differed from what Klemperer was hearing from ordinary Germans. The German command had expected to win in the U.S.S.R. before winter arrived. German troops were poorly prepared and supplied for the harsh winter. They reached as far north as Leningrad (now St. Petersburg), but never conquered the U.S.S.R.

NOW YOU KNOW

• The German invasion of the Soviet Union began in June 1941.

• The Soviets were taken by surprise and suffered huge losses.

• Soviet resistance to the invasion reorganized and became more effective.

Life on the Home Front

WARTIME EUROPE HAD A POPULATION OF 500 MILLION PEOPLE. While armies bombed and fought to control the continent, more civilians were killed than soldiers. In countries under Nazi rule, ordinary people—especially Jews—worked as slaves in work camps and prisons. In Poland, men, women, and children were regularly rounded up in such public places as movie theaters and sent to Germany as slave labor. The conditions of these camps were terrible, and many people died. In war-torn areas, shortages of food plagued civilian populations. Food shortages in some parts of Europe led to the deaths of thousands.

▲ British women and children stand in line for ration coupons—coupons that allowed the holder a limited amount of an item, such as milk or bread. In some countries, food shortages during the war led to mass starvation. Over the winter of 1944 and spring of 1945 in the Netherlands, about 16,000 civilians starved to death. In the spring of 1945, Dutch weekly rations were 14 ounces (400 grams) of bread (about half a small loaf) and 18 ounces (500 grams) of potatoes or beets. Hundreds of thousands starved in the Soviet Union during the war (see pages 26-27).

▶ This notice appeared in every hotel bathroom in the United Kingdom from October 1942. U.S. First Lady Eleanor Roosevelt (1884-1962) stated that the notice was even posted in her guest-room bath in Buckingham Palace.

As part of your personal share in the Battle for Fuel you are asked NOT to exceed 5 inches [13 centimeters] of water in this bath . . .

Make it a point of honour [the British spelling of honor] not to fill the bath above this level.

notice in the United Kingdom, 1942

3

Zusatz-Lebensmittelkarte
für Hochzeiten

3 Personen

Ernährungsamt Berlin

47066

29.9.44

Ausgegeben am

Nicht übertragbar! Nur gültig für die Dauer von 14 Tagen
Abtrennen nur durch Empfänger der Abschnitte

◀ A ration card (in German, *Lebensmittelkarte,* or food card) from Germany. Such cards allowed people certain amounts of sugar, meat, and other things in short supply during World War II. Food was scarce and ration cards were used in both Europe and the United States during the war. Other scarce supplies, such as clothing and gasoline, were also rationed.

▶ An American aid worker, in Stalingrad to distribute food soon after the battle, describes the surviving children, in Antony Beevor's history *Stalingrad* (1998). The Soviet city of Stalingrad (now Volgograd) was the site of fierce fighting between the German and Soviet armies (see also pages 30-31). Much of the city's large population was caught in the crossfire. During lulls in the fighting, civilians came out of holes in the ground to cut meat from dead horses. At night, orphaned children *scavenged* (picked over) bombed grain-storage buildings for burned wheat.

4

Most of the children had been living in the ground for four or five winter months. They were swollen with hunger. They *cringed* [shrank back] in corners, afraid to speak, to even look people in the face.

an American aid worker, 1943

NOW YOU KNOW

- Ration cards were issued to distribute precious food and supplies during the war.
- Nazis used civilians as slave labor.
- Civilians suffered terribly during the war.

A World at War

O N DEC. 7, 1941, THE JAPANESE ATTACKED THE UNITED STATES PACIFIC FLEET at Pearl Harbor, Hawaii. The United States—already a crucial supplier to the Allies—declared war on Japan. By the summer of 1942, World War II had swallowed up nearly all of Europe and spread to many other parts of the world. Nazi Germany controlled most of Europe, and Hitler's plan for a German empire seemed close to success.

1

This outcome of the struggle has not been decided by the Battle of France. This is a world war.

Charles
de Gaulle, 1940

◄ General Charles de Gaulle (1890-1970), a leader of the French resistance, stressed the worldwide nature of the war in a 1940 BBC radio broadcast from London. This speech is known as the *Appeal of June 18*. When France surrendered to Germany, a new, Nazi-controlled government—known as the Vichy government—was formed in the south of the country. Many French people—including de Gaulle—rejected this government. De Gaulle escaped to the United Kingdom, where he organized and led the Free French Forces opposed to German rule. In this speech, he called on members of the French military to join him in the United Kingdom and fight on.

2

▲ United States President Franklin D. Roosevelt (1882-1945) sits (above, left) next to British Prime Minister Winston Churchill on August 1941, aboard the U.S.S. *Augusta* off the coast of the Canadian island of Newfoundland. At this conference the leaders created the Atlantic Charter—a document that strengthened their alliance and outlined the goals following an Allied victory. The Atlantic Charter became the basis of the Declaration by United Nations—a first step toward the modern UN—in January 1942.

3

A few of us passing into the Strait of Gibraltar on a *Liberty Ship* [U.S. cargo ship] are pretty thoughtful. Just what are we doing 4,000 miles [6,450 kilometers] from home? Are we defending something very real and personal or are we being sacrificed on the same old altar of greed and ambition? In this war, the soldier has no choice but to do or die. . . .

an American soldier remembers his feelings in 1942

▲ Germany declared war on the United States in December 1941, but many Americans still felt it wasn't their fight. As this soldier states in Joseph E. Garland's *Unknown Soldiers* (2008), not all Americans were sure why they were risking their lives.

► A U.S. poster encouraged women to help the war effort by taking jobs traditionally done by men.

4

The more WOMEN at work the sooner we WIN!

WOMEN ARE NEEDED ALSO AS:

FARM WORKERS	WAITRESSES	TIMEKEEPERS	LAUNDRESSES
TYPISTS	BUS DRIVERS	ELEVATOR OPERATORS	TEACHERS
SALESPEOPLE	TAXI DRIVERS	MESSENGERS	CONDUCTORS

— and in hundreds of other war jobs!

SEE YOUR LOCAL U.S. EMPLOYMENT SERVICE

NOW YOU KNOW

- Charles de Gaulle led the Free French movement against Nazi rule.
- The Atlantic Charter became the basis of the Declaration by United Nations.
- In the summer of 1942, Germany was at the height of its military success.

The Siege of Leningrad

In September 1941, German armies surrounded the Russian city of Leningrad (now St. Petersburg). Nearly all supplies were cut off. The more than 2 million citizens and soldiers of Leningrad held out as best they could, suffering through winters without electric power and enduring shortages of water, food, and medicine—all the while under bombardment by German *artillery* (heavy guns). The Leningrad *siege* (surrounding of the city and preventing movement in or out of it) lasted 872 days. The Red Army broke through and freed the city in January 1944. Historians think perhaps as many as 1.7 million Soviet people, both military and civilians, died in and around Leningrad during the siege. A great many of them died of starvation. But, the defense of the city held. Had Leningrad fallen, it would have been much easier for the Germans to have conquered the Soviet capital of Moscow.

▶ At the onset of the siege, Adolf Hitler made clear his hatred of the Soviets and his determination to crush Leningrad, in a conversation he held with a German ambassador published in Michael Jones's history *Leningrad: State of Siege* (2008).

Petersburg [Leningrad]—the poisonous nest from which, for so long, Asiatic *venom* [hatred] has spewed forth into the Baltic—must vanish from the earth's surface. The city is already cut off. It only remains for us to bomb and bombard it, destroy its sources of water and power and then deny the population everything it needs to survive.

Adolf Hitler, 1941

◀ An ice road across frozen Lake Ladoga. The lake, to the northeast of Leningrad, provided a lifeline to the city. When it froze in winter, it allowed the Soviets to create a road over the lake, between a rail station held by the Soviets on one shore and Leningrad to the south. Desperately needed supplies were brought in across the ice. When the lake was unfrozen in summer, boats were used to move supplies. But it was never enough. By spring of 1942, more than half a million people had starved in Leningrad.

3

◀ A cabbage patch before Saint Isaac's Cathedral in Leningrad. Food was grown in the center of Leningrad during the siege. At first, the food allowance there was 28 ounces (800 grams) per day. By the winter of 1941-1942, it was 8 ounces (250 grams) per day for manual workers and 4 ounces (125 grams) per day for other civilians. During that winter, people passed corpses laying where they had died nearly every time they walked down the street. The number of people dying of starvation was huge, and many times the living were too weak with hunger to take the dead to a cemetery to be buried.

NOW YOU KNOW

- The Nazis surrounded Leningrad and tried to starve the city into surrender.
- Despite terrible hardship, the people of Leningrad held out for more than 2 years.
- Some 1.7 million Soviets died during the siege.

Soldiers at War

SOLDIERS FROM ALL CORNERS OF THE GLOBE—MORE THAN 50 NATIONS—fought in World War II, and many died on the battlefields of Europe. Most soldiers came from ordinary backgrounds and were *conscripted* (drafted) into the military. Once drafted, they often went through schools and training to prepare them for battle. It took many different kinds of soldiers to make an army. Aside from combat duties, soldiers served as clerks, cooks, doctors, drivers, engineers, guards, mechanics, medics, military policemen, pilots, radio operators, and technicians—even artists. Some of the fighters who served in World War II were not in a regular army. Their nation had already fallen to the enemy, so they did their fighting with an irregular army, or resistance movement. About 70 million people served in the armed forces of the Allied and Axis nations. About 20 million of them lost their lives.

1

One of the soldiers yelled out that he had been hit. I went up and saw that he had caught a piece of *shrapnel* [exploded shell]. It just missed a vein but shattered his leg. While I was attending to him, George ran back to the *CP* [Command Post] and got a couple of guys with a *litter* [stretcher] and came back to where I was. We got this fellow on the litter and the four of us carried him. On the way back . . . the Germans lobbed in a couple of *mortar* [small cannon] shells. George got hit with a *fragment* [piece] across the *temple* [side of the head]. He died in our arms; he just bled to death. He kept asking us, "Please help me, please help me." There wasn't a thing we could do.

Allen Bedard describes events in 1944

◀ On March 24, 1944, U.S. Army Corporal George Sylvester Viereck, Jr., was killed by enemy fire. A friend, Corporal Allen Bedard, describes the event in an interview published in *The Rock of Anzio* (1998).

2

▶ African-American soldiers from the 92nd Infantry Division—the famous "Buffalo Soldiers." They fought in Italy in 1944 through 1945. After the Japanese attack on Pearl Harbor, hundreds of thousands of African Americans volunteered or were drafted into the U.S. military. They were not allowed to serve with white Americans. They were only able to serve in special all-black units.

◀ Polish troops serving in the United Kingdom's army. After Poland fell to Nazi Germany, many Poles who escaped the country fought for other Allied armies.

4

▶ The Jan. 25, 1943, issue of *Time* magazine published a Yugoslav father's letter to his child. The man joined a resistance group after German troops invaded his country in 1941. He was shot some weeks later. Knowing he was about to die, he wrote these words to his unborn son.

My child, sleeping now in the dark and gathering strength for the struggle of birth, I wish you well. . . .

Keep your heart hungry for new knowledge; keep your hatred of a lie; and keep your power of *indignation* [anger at something unworthy].

Now I know I must die, and you must be born to stand upon the rubbish-heap of my errors. Forgive me for this. I am ashamed to leave you an untidy, uncomfortable world. But so it must be.

In thought, as a last *benediction* [blessing], I kiss your forehead. Goodnight to you—and good morning and a clear dawn.

Time, 1943

DOCUMENTING *magazine*

NOW YOU KNOW

- More than 50 nations participated in World War II.
- It took many different types of soldiers to keep an army running.
- About 20 million soldiers died during the war.

Stalingrad: Germany Halted

IN THE SPRING OF 1942, GERMAN ARMIES ADVANCED TOWARD OIL FIELDS deep within the Soviet Union. Hitler ordered his troops to take the city of Stalingrad (now Volgograd)—named for Joseph Stalin, the Soviet dictator. The battle for the city began in August and was one of the largest and bloodiest in history. Around 1 million Axis and Soviet troops died there, along with hundreds of thousands of civilians. In the end, it was a brutal German defeat and proved to be the turning point in the war on the *Eastern Front* (the battle line in eastern Europe).

◀ A painting of the street fighting between German and Soviet troops in the Soviet city of Stalingrad. The savage Battle of Stalingrad began in August 1942 and dragged on for five months. The Germans took most of the city but could not hold it. Neighborhoods, city blocks, even individual buildings were fought over for days or weeks, leaving thousands of people dead. Then the same areas of buildings were fought over again, as the sides advanced and retreated.

▶ Joseph Stalin's order forbidding surrender was read to all troops in the Red Army in mid-1942.

Panic-mongers [people creating fear] and cowards must be destroyed on the spot. The retreat *mentality* [way of thinking] must be decisively *eliminated* [stopped]. Army commanders who have allowed the voluntary abandonment of positions must be removed and sent for immediate trial by military *tribunal* [court].

Joseph Stalin, 1942

3

▲ Statue of Soviet dictator Joseph Stalin. During his more than 20 years in power, he ordered millions of Soviet citizens to be executed or sent to labor camps. Before the war, many officers were caught up in these *purges,* which hampered the Soviet war effort.

4

"When the time comes, we will commit suicide."

"Suicide?"

"Yes, *Herr* [Sir] General! My colonel will also shoot himself. He believes we should not allow ourselves to be captured."

"Well let me tell you something. You will not shoot yourself, nor will your colonel shoot himself. You will go into captivity along with your men and will do everything you can to set a good example."

General Karl Strecker describes a conversation in Stalingrad in 1943

▲ Soviet troops counterattacked in the Battle of Stalingrad in mid-November, 1942; eventually trapping the German Army. Each day, thousands of German soldiers froze, starved to death, or died of disease. On Feb. 2, 1943, after months of suffering, the last German troops in Stalingrad surrendered. Hitler had ordered his generals to commit suicide rather than accept defeat. German General Karl Strecker, however, felt there was nothing dishonorable about surrendering when defeat was certain.

NOW YOU KNOW

- The Battle of Stalingrad was one of the bloodiest battles in history.
- The battle was a turning point in the war on the Eastern Front.
- The Germans were defeated, and Stalingrad remained in Soviet hands.

The Death Camps

B Y 1942, HITLER HAD BEGUN THE MASS MURDER OF EUROPEAN JEWS—which became known as the *Holocaust*. Many of the Holocaust victims were killed in specially constructed gas chambers, and their bodies were then burned. The word *holocaust* means something offered in a sacrifice that is completely burned. The Nazis rounded up Jewish men, women, and children from occupied Europe and shipped them in railway cars to concentration camps, where they were killed or used as slave labor. Hitler's forces killed around 6 million European Jews, half of whom were Polish—60 percent of Europe's prewar Jewish population. The Nazis also slaughtered clergy of Christian religions, Slavs (particularly Poles and Soviet prisoners of war), Roma (sometimes called Gypsies), socialists, communists, homosexuals, and developmentally disabled people.

▲ Hungarian Jews arrive at Auschwitz, in Poland, in June 1944. Note that some wear the star that, by law, the Nazis forced them to wear to identify their religion (see page 17). More than 1 million people, mostly Jews, were killed at Auschwitz. Other victims included Poles, Roma, and Soviet prisoners of war.

2

It was dark, a blue light was shining on the platform. We saw a few *S.S. men* [members of Hitler's security force] walking up and down. They separated the men from the women. . . . I could see my wife there with the child in her arms. . . . A truck arrived, stopped near us and on the truck were all the women, children, babies and in the centre [British spelling] my wife and child standing up. They stood up to the light as if it was meant to be like that—so that I could recognize them. A picture I'll never forget. All these were supposed to have gone to the bathroom to have a bath, to eat and to live. Instead they had to undress and go into the gas chambers, and two hours later those people were ashes, including my wife and child.

Leon Greenman describes Auschwitz in 1943

◀ A British Jew, Leon Greenman (1910-2008), recalls his experience in an interview published in Lyn Smith's *Remembering: Voices of the Holocaust* (2005). Greenman was captured by the Nazis while living in the Netherlands and sent to Auschwitz in 1943.

At Auschwitz, people arrived in packed train cars. Such people as Greenman who were strong enough to work were separated out. The rest were immediately taken to what looked like showers. Instead of water, however, poison gas was released into the room, killing everyone inside. Afterward, the bodies of the dead were generally burned in special buildings known as *crematoria*.

3

I had a dream,
A dream so terrible:
My people were no more,
No more!

I wake up with a cry,
What I dreamed was true:
It happened indeed,
It had happened to me.

from *The Song of the Murdered Jewish People* (1943), Yitzhak Katzenelson

▶ A verse from Yitzhak Katzenelson (1886-1944), a Jewish teacher and poet who grew up in Poland. His wife and two sons died in the Treblinka death camp in occupied Poland. He and his other son fought in the Warsaw ghetto uprising (see page 48) before escaping to France. Knowing he was in danger, he hid his writings. In 1944, he and his son were sent to Auschwitz and killed. His writings were found and published after the war.

NOW YOU KNOW

- The Nazi effort to murder European Jews and others became known as the Holocaust.
- Half of the 6 million Jews killed by the Nazis were Polish.
- Roma, socialists, communists, homosexuals, and developmentally disabled people were also Holocaust victims.

Women in Combat

IN MOST COUNTRIES, INCLUDING GERMANY, THE UNITED KINGDOM, and the United States, women were not allowed to serve in combat. Nevertheless, military women in World War II faced extreme danger as nurses, who were often very close to combat. Women from Germany and the United Kingdom also served in antiaircraft units. British women were also required to register with the government as of 1941, and then to choose among jobs considered essential to the war effort. By 1943, more than 80 percent of British women were working in such essential jobs. In the United States, women were not required to register, but many women did work in wartime jobs. In the Soviet Union, women were allowed into combat, and around 8 million Soviet women joined military units. All-women combat units were formed in the Red, or Soviet, Army and Red Air Force. Many Soviet women in the military were employed as truck drivers, doctors, and even combat pilots. Women from Allied nations served in anti-Nazi resistance movements.

1

Right until the late afternoon we had to fight, shot for shot, against thirty-seven enemy anti-aircraft positions, manned by *tenacious* [stubborn] fighting women, until they were all destroyed.

> a German soldier
> describes fighting at
> Stalingrad in 1942

▲ A German soldier recalls an attack during the Battle of Stalingrad (see pages 30-31) in Antony Beevor's history *Stalingrad*. The most famous all-women unit of the Soviet Air Force was the 46th Guards Light Night Bomber Regiment. This German attack was on that unit's antiaircraft gunners.

▶ A Soviet poster from World War II reads, "Put all the country's efforts into defeating the enemy." The Soviet Union used both men and women in combat and to produce war materials.

2

Все силы народа на разгром врага!

34

3

A second direct hit again brought it [the tank] to a standstill, but in spite of its hopeless position the T-34 defended itself until a tank killer team advanced on it. Finally it burst into flames from a *demolition charge* [a type of explosive used to penetrate steel], and only then did the turret hatch open. A woman in a Red Army tanker uniform climbed out. She was the wife and crewmember of the Russian tank company commander who, killed by the first hit, lay beside her in the turret.

German General Erhard Raus

◀ German General Erhard Raus recalls an attack on a Russian tank with a woman soldier aboard during the invasion of the Soviet Union, in a work published after the war.

▼ Armed Italians helping Allied troops hunt for German soldiers in September 1944. Experts estimate that one in three Italian *partisans*—resistance fighters not in the regular army—were women. Women also joined resistance forces in France and Yugoslavia and a large number joined anti-Nazi resistance groups in Greece. The British Secret Service also used women to enter Nazi-occupied France and work with the French resistance.

4

NOW YOU KNOW

- During World War II, most countries did not allow women to fight in combat.
- Around 8 million Soviet women joined fighting units.
- Many women joined partisan groups in occupied Europe, especially in France, Greece, Italy, and Yugoslavia.

The Invasion of Italy

IN 1943, THE ALLIES WERE NOT YET READY TO INVADE FRANCE. The British wanted to invade Italy to make the Mediterranean safe for the transport of oil from the Middle East and India. Allied forces landed on the Italian island of Sicily in July 1943. In that same month, Italian dictator Benito Mussolini was removed from power by members of the Italian government. However, Mussolini remained in control of northern Italy, which was occupied by German troops. In September 1943, Allied forces landed at Salerno, Italy, just after the Italian government formally surrendered to the Allies. The Germans, however, refused to give up Italy and fought the Allies fiercely there until the end of the war in Europe in May 1945 (see pages 56-57).

1

> When we land against the enemy, don't forget to hit him and hit him hard. When we meet the enemy we will kill him. We will show him no mercy. He has killed thousands of your *comrades* [fellow soldiers] and he must die. . . . You will tell your men that. They must have the killer instinct. . . . We will get the name of killers and killers are immortal [never die]. When word reaches him [the enemy] that he is being faced by a killer *battalion* [army unit] he will fight less. We must build up that name as killers.
>
> General Patton, 1943

◀ American General George S. Patton is said to have addressed his officers before the July 1943 landings on Sicily with these words. Later, an American soldier who had murdered prisoners of war at Biscari, Sicily, said in his defense that he thought he was carrying out Patton's orders.

2

▶ U.S. soldiers drive tanks ashore on the Italian coast at Anzio, 30 miles (48 kilometers) from the Italian capital, Rome, in May 1944. After the Allies swarmed the beaches at Anzio in January 1944, the German forces counterattacked and there were four months of fierce fighting. More than 4,000 Allied soldiers and 5,000 Germans were killed before the Allies broke through the German lines. Rome was liberated on June 4, 1944.

3

So back we go to World War I. Oozing thick mud. Tank hulks. The cold. God, the cold. Graves marked by a helmet, gashed with shrapnel [metal fragments scattered by the explosion of an artillery shell]. Shreds of barbed wire. Trees like broken fishbones.

soldier in the Anzio trenches, 1944

◀ A soldier recorded the scene at Anzio in his diary after digging a trench with a pick and shovel. It reminded him of World War I, which had often been fought from trenches in deep mud.

4

▶ Posters made by the Allies for Italy show Franklin D. Roosevelt and Sir Winston Churchill as leaders who would free the Italian people. The bottom left poster shows a Nazi officer with the words "This is the Enemy!" The bottom right poster shows a German boot ready to stamp on a map of Italy.

NOW YOU KNOW

- Allied troops began the invasion of Italy in July 1943.
- Dictator Benito Mussolini fell from power over southern Italy in July 1943.
- German forces fought for control of Italy until the end of the war.

The Propaganda War

PROPAGANDA IS ONE-SIDED COMMUNICATION DESIGNED TO INFLUENCE people's thinking and actions. All the warring nations in World War II used propaganda to win support for their policies. Governments aimed propaganda both at their own people and at the enemy. Radio broadcasts reached the largest audiences, but motion pictures, posters, and cartoons were also used.

1

You have been told the war would end in autumn. . . . Quite a number of your fellows, however, have *kicked the bucket* [died]. Pretty tough for the replacements who never dreamt of having to cross *the pond* [Atlantic Ocean] isn't it?

a German leaflet dropped over U.S. troops, 1945

2

▲ Propaganda leaflets, first dropped by the British over German towns and cities, were used by all sides. This message, designed to discourage enemy soldiers, is from a German propaganda leaflet that was dropped over American troops in Germany in 1945.

◀ A U.S. propaganda poster promotes the idea of a world united against the Axis powers. The flags of four chief Allies—the United Kingdom, the United States, China, and the Soviet Union (left to right)— encircle the barrels of large artillery guns. The flags of other Allies (Norway to the far left and Australia to the far right) can be partly seen. The remaining gun barrels represent still more Allies.

▶ Propaganda for the Hitler Youth movement (see page 7) included this verse in its *anthem* (song of loyalty). The anthem was written by Hitler Youth leader Baldur von Schirach (1907-1974) for a 1934 propaganda film.

3

We march for Hitler
Through night and need
With the flag of youth for freedom and bread.
Our flag *unfurls* [unfolds] before us.
Our flag is the new time.
And our flag leads us into eternity!
Yes, our flag is more than death.

Hitler Youth anthem

DAKAR-MERS EL-KEBIR

◀ A propaganda poster. When France fell to German forces, the Vichy government, which supported the Nazis, was established (see page 24). The Vichy government created this poster showing a shadowy Sir Winston Churchill as responsible for killing French sailors. The United Kingdom had feared that French naval ships would fall under Nazi control. The French Navy had ships at anchor at Dakar in West Africa and Mers-el-Kebir in North Africa. The French Navy refused to surrender their ships to the British or disarm them when requested. The British forces attacked and successfully destroyed the French fleet at Mers-el-Kebir. The crosses in the lower right corner of the poster refer to the 1,297 French sailors who were killed in this action.

NOW YOU KNOW

- Propaganda is one-sided communication designed to influence people's thinking and actions.
- All the warring nations used propaganda during World War II.
- Leaflets dropped on enemy territory and public posters in the home country were common forms of propaganda.

War Movies

URING WORLD WAR II, MANY MOVIES WERE MADE BY the larger warring nations—especially the United Kingdom and the United States. These movies showed British and American troops fighting with great heroism against the evils of the Axis nations. The war movies told stories of glory, sacrifice, and the miracles of Allied production—thousands of tanks, warplanes, warships, and endless guns. Such movies as *Mrs. Miniver* (1942) and *Since You Went Away* (1944) showed life on the home front. Since the end of World War II in 1945, war movies have continued to tell the many stories from all sides of the conflict in Europe. Often, newer war movies are less *biased* (in favor of one side) and instead try to focus on the horrors of war suffered by all soldiers.

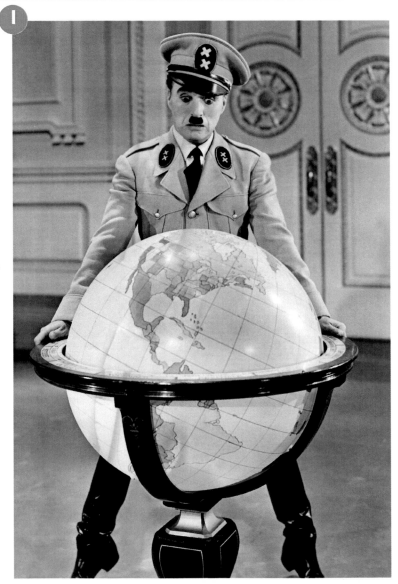

► British actor and comedian Charlie Chaplin (1889-1977) ridicules Adolf Hitler in *The Great Dictator* (1940). The movie was shown in the United States before that nation entered the war. In one well-known scene, Chaplin plays a character patterned after Hitler and dances with a large, inflatable globe. The Hitler-like character can only think of ruling the world.

2

Rick Blaine: Don't you sometimes wonder if it's worth all this? I mean what you're fighting for.

Victor Laszlo: You might as well question why we breathe. If we stop breathing, we'll die. If we stop fighting our enemies, the world will die.

Rick Blaine: Well, what of it? It'll be out of its misery.

Victor Laszlo: You know how you sound, Mr. Blaine? Like a man who's trying to convince himself of something he doesn't believe in his heart.

from *Casablanca*

▲ *Casablanca* (1942), set in the North African port of the title, starred American actor Humphrey Bogart (1899-1957) and Swedish actress Ingrid Bergman (1915-1982). In 1942, North Africa was ruled in name by the Vichy French, but in reality Nazi Germany was controlling the region. *Casablanca* features an anti-Nazi resistance fighter, Victor Laszlo, who is wanted by the Germans and must escape North Africa to survive. Rick Blaine, an American bar owner played by Bogart, helps Laszlo, but at great personal cost.

▶ *The Longest Day* (1962) starred many famous actors, including American John Wayne (1907-1979). The movie is based on the Allied invasion of Normandy in northern France in June 1944—known as D-Day (see pages 46-47). The film's title comes from a speech made by German General Erwin Rommel to a group of his generals as they look across the English Channel.

3

Just look at it, gentlemen. How calm . . . how peaceful it is. A strip of water between England and the continent . . . between the Allies and us. But beyond that peaceful horizon . . . a monster waits. A coiled spring of men, ships, and planes . . . straining to be released against us. But, gentlemen, not a single Allied soldier shall reach the shore. Whenever and wherever this invasion may come, gentlemen . . . I shall destroy the enemy there, at the water's edge. Believe me, gentlemen, the first 24 hours of the invasion will be decisive. For the Allies as well as the Germans, it will be the longest day.

from *The Longest Day*

NOW YOU KNOW

• War movies made during and soon after World War II tended to focus on the glory of war.

• Charlie Chaplin played a character patterned on Adolf Hitler in *The Great Dictator*.

• Modern war movies are more likely to tell stories featuring the suffering of war.

Tanks at War

TANKS OFTEN MEANT THE DIFFERENCE BETWEEN VICTORY AND DEFEAT on the battlefields of World War II. Tanks got their name from the British, who developed them during World War I and first used them against the Germans in 1916. While these early vehicles were being built, the British called them "water tanks" to conceal their purpose. During World War II, tanks ruled the desert plains of North Africa in 1942. In 1943, near the Russian city of Kursk, hundreds of German and Soviet tanks fought a huge tank battle. During the invasion known as D-Day, tanks that were able to float tried to clear a path for the Allied soldiers who landed on the beaches of Normandy.

▲ Soviet T-34 tanks advancing during the Battle of Kursk in July 1943. The Soviets successfully halted the German advance into Russia.

▶ Nikita Khrushchev (1894-1971), who would become leader of the Soviet Union in 1958, described the Battle of Kursk in his autobiography. Khrushchev was a political officer with the Red Army during the battle.

2

. . . when the enemy offensive began, we had approximately 2,500 tanks. That was an enormous power! Our intelligence services reported that the enemy [Germans] had approximately the same number of tanks. This meant that on this narrow sector of the battlefront, taking the one side and the other together, there was a total of between four and five thousand [tanks] . . . we were waiting expectantly. We were confident that we would be successful.

Nikita Khrushchev
describes Kursk in 1943

3

4

Tanks mean advances of miles at a time, not yards.

Percy Hobart, on the value of tanks over artillery

◀ British Major General Sir Percy Hobart (1885-1957) was an early supporter of tanks, but more cautious members of the British War Office could not see the value of armored vehicles. Hobart was forced to retire from the British Army in 1940, but by 1943, the wisdom of his ideas about tanks began to be understood. He was given command of Britain's 79th Armoured Division in 1943. The division contained engineers, and they made changes to ordinary tanks to adapt them to special situations. For example, they adapted tanks, such as the one shown at left, with an attachment that exploded mines before the tank got too near.

NOW YOU KNOW

- Tanks played an important role on the battlefields of Europe.
- A large tank battle took place near the Russian city of Kursk in 1943.
- Tanks played an important part during the Normandy invasion on D-Day in 1944.

The Allies Fight Back

After the 1943 Battle of Kursk, Nazi forces began to retreat back toward Germany. They crossed the Dnieper River in eastern Europe, pursued by Soviet forces determined to recover the Ukraine. In western Europe, the Allies agreed that an invasion of northern France would take place in the summer of 1944. Germany, already fighting huge battles in the east, was about to be attacked from the west.

▶ As a German soldier explains in a letter home to his wife, Nazi forces were ordered to destroy anything that might be of use to the enemy. The German forces were withdrawing across the Dnieper River (in present-day Ukraine) in September 1943, and they hoped the destruction would slow the advance of Soviet troops.

1

On the other side of the river everything has been burning fiercely for days already, for you must know that all the towns and villages in the areas that we are now evacuating [leaving] are being set ablaze, even the smallest house in the village has to go. All the large buildings are being blown up. The Russians are to find nothing but a field of rubble [broken stones and bricks]. This deprives them of every possibility of accommodating [housing and feeding] their troops. So it's a horrifyingly beautiful picture.

German soldier, 1943

2

◀ Jeeps loaded with supplies. Over a period of six months, some 2 million Americans and Canadians arrived in the United Kingdom to take part in the planned invasion of France. Huge amounts of weapons and equipment, such as these jeeps, were brought from factories in the United States.

3

Already in May, even in April, we were expecting an invasion. It was the subject of daily conversation. It was known that the British troops were being trained for a large invasion. We read in the papers, the German papers and Swiss papers, that Stalin was urgently in need of another [battle] front . . . . We sat there and thought, well, this is where it will be.

German soldier describes the situation in France in 1944

▲ An interview published after the war shows that Helmut Liebeskind, a German soldier on duty in northern France, had little doubt that an Allied invasion from the sea was only a matter of time in 1944.

▶ Allied forces liberate the city of Rome in June 1944. In the front passenger seat of the jeep is U.S. Lieutenant General Mark Clark (1896-1984), who commanded the Allied troops that fought for Rome. German troops continued to fight in some areas of Italy until the war ended in 1945.

4

NOW YOU KNOW

- In the second half of 1943, German forces began retreating from Russia.
- The Allies planned for an invasion of France in mid-1944.
- Allied forces liberated Rome in June 1944, but the Germans continued to fight in some areas of Italy until the war's end.

D-Day: The Allies in France

THE GERMANS EXPECTED AN INVASION FROM THE SEA, but they did not know exactly where or when it would occur. From April to June 1944, Allied bombers hit targets in France and Germany to weaken resistance to the coming invasion. On June 6, the D-Day invasion began. As more than 100,000 Allied troops landed on the beaches of Normandy in northwestern France, some 20,000 Allied soldiers dropped farther inland by parachute and glider. By the end of June, about 1 million Allied troops had reached France.

1

◀ American and British planners of the Normandy invasion. Standing from left to right are U.S. general Omar Bradley (1893-1981); British admiral Sir Bertram Ramsay (1883-1945); the head of the RAF, Sir Trafford Leigh-Mallory (1892-1944); and U.S. general Walter Bedell Smith (1895-1961), Dwight Eisenhower's Chief of Staff. Seated from left to right are Sir Arthur Tedder (1890-1967), a senior commander of the RAF; U.S. general Dwight D. Eisenhower, (1890-1969); and British Field Marshal Sir Bernard Montgomery (1887-1976).

2

▶ General Dwight D. Eisenhower explains his decision to change the date of the D-Day invasion in the Dec. 13, 1948, issue of *Time* magazine.

At three-thirty the next morning our little camp was shaking and shuddering under a wind of almost hurricane proportions and the accompanying rain seemed to be traveling in horizontal streaks. . . . the first report . . . was that the bad conditions predicted the day before for the coast of France were actually *prevailing* [happening] there and that if we had *persisted* [continued] in the attempt to land on June 5 a major disaster would most surely have resulted. This they probably told us to *inspire* [create] more confidence in their next *astonishing declaration* [amazing statement], which was that by the following morning a period of relatively good weather, heretofore completely unexpected, would *ensue* [occur], lasting probably thirty-six hours. . . . I quickly announced the decision to go ahead with the attack on June 6. The time was then 4:15 a.m., June 5. No one present disagreed.

Time, 1948

DOCUMENTING *magazine*

3

Even so the boat containing assault [attack] unit Company G, which I commanded, took a direct hit from the artillery of the Germans, and I suffered major casualties . . . . As soon as we were able to assemble we proceeded off the beach through a minefield which had been identified by some of the soldiers who had landed earlier. We knew this because two of them were lying there in the path I selected. Both men had been destroyed by the mines. From their position, however, we were able to identify the path and get through the minefield without casualties and proceed up to the crest [high point] of the ridge which overlooked the beach.

Captain Joseph T. Dawson,
1944

◀ U.S. Army Captain Joseph T. Dawson (1914-1998) describes the landing on Omaha Beach in a journal of his war experiences. Omaha was a code name for an American landing place at Normandy. The fighting on Omaha Beach was by far the worst. Landing craft had been *swamped* (filled with water) in rough seas, so the Allies did not have the tanks and men for which they had planned. The beach was overlooked by cliffs, and at their top the German forces had built a system of connected trenches, "resistance nests," and concrete fortifications with artillery. They had also placed mines on the beach. Some 2,500 American troops died at Omaha Beach in the fighting.

4

▶ Flat-bottomed landing craft specially designed and built for beach landings. Doors at the front of the craft swung open to allow troops to step into the shallow water. A ramp allowed vehicles to be landed, as well.

NOW YOU KNOW

- The invasion of northern France began on June 6, 1944.
- More than 100,000 Allied troops hit the beaches on D-Day.
- The landings were successful, despite difficulties at Omaha Beach.

Civilian Resistance

ROM 1940 TO 1944, NAZI GERMANY OCCUPIED MOST OF EUROPE. Some people in the occupied countries worked with the Nazis, reporting Jews who were then rounded up and sent to concentration camps. These people were known as collaborators. There were many others, however—even in Germany—who risked their lives to work against the Nazis. People throughout Europe joined *underground resistance* (secret opposition) groups. Resistance fighters, or *partisans*, damaged Nazi supplies and transportation, ambushed German soldiers, helped Jewish families, gathered information for the Allies, and helped Allied pilots who had been shot down to escape from enemy territory. Organized resistance in Belgium, Denmark, France, Greece, the Netherlands, Yugoslavia, and other countries greatly helped the Allied cause and saved thousands of lives.

▲ German soldiers arrest Jews during the destruction of the ghetto in Warsaw (see also pages 17 and 33). The Jews learned that people who were rounded up and deported from the Warsaw ghetto were being sent to their death in concentration camps. Feeling they had nothing to lose, the Warsaw Jews decided to fight. The uprising began on April 19, 1943. Lightly armed Jewish fighters stopped the Germans for four weeks. On May 16, the Germans crushed the resistance and burned the ghetto to the ground. Thousands of Jews died in the uprising. Almost all of the surviving Jews in the ghetto were sent to concentration camps.

▶ A woman recalls her time as a French resistance fighter in an interview published after the war. Finding supplies and shelter was one type of work done for the resistance movement.

2 We had to hide the *escapees* [people who had escaped] while waiting for a plane to pick them up and take them to London. For some we had to find hospital beds and medical supplies. Women were better suited for this work. They were more secure, less suspect. Women know how to solve these problems. They were not that different from the problems women have to deal with all the time.

French partisan

3 No one returned of those marched through the gates of the ghetto. All the roads of the *Gestapo* [Nazi police force] lead to Ponar. And Ponar means death. Those who *waver* [hesitate], put aside all *illusion* [mistaken ideas]. Your children, your wives, and husbands are no more. . . . All were shot dead there [in Ponar]. Hitler conspires to kill all the Jews of Europe, and the Jews of Lithuania have been picked at the first line. Let us not be led as sheep to the slaughter!

Abba Kovner, 1942

◀ A speech by Jewish poet Abba Kovner (1918-1987) encouraging resistance. Kovner lived in the ghetto established by the Nazis in Vilnius (then called Vilna), Lithuania. In 1942, after the murder of 6,000 Jews at Ponar, outside Vilna, Kovner helped to form a resistance group that carried out attacks against the Nazis.

NOW YOU KNOW

- Some people *collaborated with* (helped) the Nazis, but many others risked their lives to work against them.
- Resistance fighters greatly helped the Allied cause.
- Resistance groups developed in most Nazi-occupied countries over the course of the war.

Bombing Germany

B Y MAY 1941, GERMANY HAD LARGELY STOPPED ITS BOMBING OF THE UNITED KINGDOM. But Allied bombers pounded Germany until the end of the war. Raids of more than 1,000 Allied bombers targeted cities all over Germany. One of the cities worst hit was Dresden. Dresden was a city of great beauty and culture. It had not prepared for bombings, and around 25,000 people died in Allied raids in 1945. The Allies believed that the bombing of German cities would destroy the enemy's industrial base as well as its desire and ability to go on fighting. This did not happen until very late in the war. Some 150,000 Allied aviators were killed in the bombing raids, along with perhaps as many as 500,000 German civilians.

◀ Civilians carrying water in the ruins of the German city of Mannheim in April 1945. Entire cities were destroyed in the bombing raids.

▶ Traute Koch, a 15-year-old schoolgirl in 1943, describes the bombing of Hamburg in July of that year, in a work published after the war. The German port city was destroyed by a series of raids that left more than 40,000 people dead and 1 million homeless.

Mother wrapped me in wet sheets, kissed me, and said, "Run!" I hesitated at the door in front of me . . . I could only see fire—everything red like the door to a furnace. An intense heat struck me. . . . Someone came out, grabbed me in their arms, and pulled me into the doorway. I screamed for my mother and somebody gave me a drink. . . .

I still screamed and then my mother and my little sister were there. About 20 people had gathered in the cellar. We sat holding tightly to each other and waited. My mother wept bitterly and I was terrified.

Traute Koch describes the bombing of Hamburg in 1943

3

4

. . . the destruction of those cities has fatally weakened the German war effort and is now enabling Allied soldiers to advance into the heart of Germany with negligible [very few] casualties.
Arthur Harris, 1945

▲ More than 300 bombing raids destroyed much of Berlin, Germany's capital.

◀ In a letter dated March 29, 1945, Sir Arthur Harris (1892-1984), the head of the RAF Bomber Command, defends the bombing of German cities.

NOW YOU KNOW

- More than 1,000 Allied bombers were used in some Allied bombing raids.
- Entire cities were destroyed in the bombing raids.
- Some 150,000 Allied aviators and perhaps 500,000 German civilians died in the raids.

End of the Third Reich

As ALLIED FORCES ADVANCED TOWARD GERMANY IN 1944, the Soviet Red Army closed in on Germany from the east. By February 1945, Soviet troops were just 35 miles (56 kilometers) from Berlin, Germany's capital. Allied soldiers crossed the Rhine River into Germany in March 1945 under Allied Supreme Commander Dwight D. Eisenhower, as American troops swarmed into the heart of Germany. In April, Soviet and American troops met at the Elbe River near the German city of Leipzig. The war in Europe was nearly over. The Third Reich (Third Empire), as Nazi Germany had been called, was falling.

▲ U.S. soldiers captured during the Battle of the Bulge, in a photo taken by the German army. Following the successful D-Day landings in Normandy in June 1944, Allied forces advanced in Europe throughout the summer. On Dec. 16, 1944, German forces launched a major counterattack in the Ardennes Forest, which spans Belgium, France, and Luxembourg. Allied troops were forced back, causing a "bulge" in the Allied front line—the fighting that took place there is known as the Battle of the Bulge. Within two weeks, the Germans were stopped and pushed back.

▶ A diary entry written in March 1945 by a German university student from Munich.

And in this situation the [German] government is still talking of victory! In my innermost heart I too do not want to believe that our people are destined to [meant for] downfall. But if you only think about them just a little, things look very black. You can't see any chink[opening] of light any more.

German student
Lore Walb, 1945

▶ In his book *Mailed Fist* (1966), British tank commander John Foley (1917-1974) remembers crossing the German border in early 1945. Angler was the name given to one of the tanks under his command.

▼ The Red Army marches into Berlin in 1945. For weeks before, the Soviets had fought to conquer Berlin using artillery, bombs, and infantry. In some parts of the city, the conflict was waged house by house.

I stared curiously at my first German civilian. He was an old man, dressed in shabby *serge* [strong, woolen fabric] and an engine-driver's sort of cap. His *grizzled* [gray-haired] face regarded us from above a bushy white moustache as we clattered over the broken frontier barrier. And then I heard Angler's driver's hatch being thrown open, and when I looked over my shoulder I saw Smith 161 leaning out and staring questioningly at the old German. "We on the right road for Berlin, mate?" asked Smith 161, with a perfectly straight face. I swear the old blue eyes winked as the man tugged at his grizzled moustache and said: *"Berlin? Ja, ja! Gerade aus!"* [Yes, yes. Straight on.]

Mailed Fist, John Foley

NOW YOU KNOW

- The Battle of the Bulge was a large German counterattack in December 1944.
- By early 1945, Allied troops had advanced into Germany.
- In April 1945, American and Soviet troops met at the Elbe River.

Liberating the Camps

THE NAZIS RAN HUNDREDS OF DEATH AND SLAVE LABOR CAMPS throughout Germany and eastern Europe. More than half—about 3.5 million—of all Holocaust victims were killed in six death camps in Poland—Auschwitz, Belzec, Chelmno, Majdanek, Sobibor, and Treblinka. About 1.25 million people, mostly Jews, were killed at Auschwitz alone. In an effort to remove evidence of their crimes, the Nazis took apart these camps and moved most of the surviving prisoners before Soviet forces reached them in 1944. Other camps were simply abandoned. In April 1945, U.S. forces found 21,000 prisoners at Buchenwald concentration camp in Germany. In the same month, British troops discovered 60,000 survivors at the camp at Bergen-Belsen in Germany. Many prisoners died soon after liberation: They were just too ill to survive.

▶ A *replica* (a copy) made after the war of a furnace used at Auschwitz to reduce dead bodies to ash. When the Soviet Army liberated the camp, only some 7,000 prisoners remained to be freed. The Nazis had forced most of the camp's prisoners—about 60,000 people—to leave on a march westward. In their weakened state, many of them died. Soviet troops found warehouses at Auschwitz that held 836,255 women's dresses, 348,000 men's suits, and 38,000 pairs of men's shoes. It was all that remained of the murdered.

2

The people denied it. They said, "No, no, Germany didn't do this." Because that was the first time many people actually heard of concentration camps. They said, "No, this isn't true; and certainly not in our area. Oh no, no, no."

a German woman describes what was known about a local death camp

◀ A young German woman in Hamburg, living close to one of the concentration camps, recalls that local people claimed to have been unaware of the camp's existence.

3

I don't blame people who didn't come forward, but to say they didn't know what was going on is absolute rubbish: in school, in university, you knew—not exactly what happened, but that the Jews had disappeared. We thought the worse because my husband said, "If they were still alive we would hear from them." But the fact was they had disappeared, they were just not there.

a German woman describes what was thought about the fate of the Jews in the 1940's

▶ A German woman, who was a member of an anti-Hitler resistance group, states in a work published after the war that people knew that the Jews had been taken away, probably to be killed.

4

◀ Survivors of the Dachau concentration camp celebrating their liberation by U.S. troops. Dachau was the first permanent concentration camp set up by the Nazi government in Germany. Around 28,000 prisoners died at Dachau. More than 32,000 starving survivors—and 10,000 dead bodies—were found there by the Americans in late April 1945. The rest of the dead had been cremated. American soldiers were so shocked by what they saw at Dachau that for a few hours after the camp's liberation, German soldiers were murdered after surrendering to the Americans.

NOW YOU KNOW

- More than half of all Holocaust victims were killed in death camps in Poland.
- Soviet, American, and British forces liberated concentration camps in Germany and Poland.
- Survivors of the death camps were often in terrible physical condition.

The End of War in Europe

FORMER ITALIAN DICTATOR BENITO MUSSOLINI TRIED TO ESCAPE when Germany's defeat became certain. In late April 1945, he was captured and executed by Italian resistance fighters. Many German generals committed suicide in the face of defeat and, on April 30, Hitler did the same. On May 7, Germany surrendered and May 8 became V-E (Victory in Europe) Day. The end of the war was not the end of the suffering, though, as millions of persons remained homeless in Europe. They included orphans, prisoners of war, survivors of Nazi camps, and people who had fled invading armies and battlefields.

1

. . . American sailors and laughing girls formed a *conga* [dance] line down the middle of *Piccadilly* [street]. . . . Each group danced its own dance, sang its own song, and went its own way as the spirit moved it. . . . The young service men and women who swung arm in arm down the middle of every street, singing and swarming over the few cars *rash* [incautious] enough to come out, were simply happy with an *immense* [huge] holiday happiness. They were the *liberated* [free] people who, like their *counterparts* [others like them] in every celebrating capital that night, were young enough to outlive the past and to look forward to an unspoilt [British spelling of unspoiled] future. Their *gaiety* [joy] was very moving.

The New Yorker,
1945

◄ Writing for *The New Yorker* magazine, British author Mollie Panter-Downes (1906-1997) describes the scene in London on V-E Day for American readers. Mollie Panter-Downes submitted weekly articles to *The New Yorker*, titled "Letter from London," from 1939 to the end of the war (and into the 1980's).

▼ Sir Winston Churchill and the British royal family in London on V-E Day greet the public from a balcony at Buckingham Palace. Churchill, center, stands between King George VI (1895-1952) and the king's wife, Elizabeth (1900-2002). The girl on the far right is Princess Margaret (1930-2002). The young woman in uniform at left, then Princess Elizabeth, is now Queen Elizabeth II (1926-   ).

2

3

Around us fifty great cities lay in ruins. . . . Like ants in an antheap the people *scurried* [ran] over the ruins, diving *furtively* [secretly] into cellars and doorways in search of loot. . . . Life was *sordid* [dirty], aimless, leading nowhere. Every house in every unbombed village was stacked to the roof with city refugees living on soup and potatoes. . . . Every family was *bereaved* [had suffered a death] or broken up. The housing situation was impossible and likely to get worse. A very large part of the population was simply wandering on the roads with the millions of foreigners.

Alan Moorehead describes
Germany in 1945

▶ British war journalist Alan Moorehead (1910-1983) describes Germany in April 1945 in his book *Eclipse* (1945).

4

◀ Red Army troops wave the Soviet flag over the ruins of the Reichstag, the German parliament building in Berlin, on May 2, 1945. This famous photo was taken by Soviet photographer Yevgeny Khaldei.

NOW YOU KNOW

- World War II in Europe ended in May 1945.
- Mussolini was executed and Hitler committed suicide in April 1945.
- The war left millions of people homeless across Europe.

Interpreting the War

ORLD WAR II WAS THE MOST DESTRUCTIVE WAR IN HISTORY. It killed more people, destroyed more property, and disrupted more lives than any other war in history. It is impossible to say exactly how many people died as a result of World War II. Estimates suggest about 20 million soldiers died during the war's six years. Some 30 to 40 million civilians also died. Entire families, towns, and cities were destroyed. It was truly a world tragedy. Experts are still writing and thinking about the war. Novels, plays, and movies are still being made about the war as the world still attempts to understand its causes and its meaning.

▶ American author and oral historian Studs Terkel (1912–2008) holds his book, *The Good War: An Oral History of World War II*. The book records the wartime experiences of people Terkel interviewed.

[Raboud]: Very often, you hear some German saying, "We didn't know." But who allowed the Nazi to take over? They were very, very happy when Hitler took France, took Europe. At Delmenhorst [a German prison camp], we had these guards. They were married, they had families. Don't tell me when they went back home, they were not talking about what is going on. The people of Delmenhorst for pastime on Sunday were coming around the camp. They were looking at us like we were zoo animals.

[Terkel]: Is this uniquely German?

[Raboud]: This is human. It happened before. . . . It can happen again. We are all good people, but if we are led a little too far, we are going to believe everything we are told. We are ordinary people, who can also be weapons for evil Hitlers.

Jacques Raboud describes his wartime experiences

◀ In Studs Terkel's *The Good War*, Jacques Raboud, a French citizen, reflects on the Germans who held him captive. Raboud was sent to a forced-labor camp by the Nazis in 1943. By the time he was liberated by American forces in 1945, Raboud weighed 80 pounds (36 kilograms) and was near death. Years later, when interviewed, he discussed the capability ordinary people have for evil.

3

Orders came for sailing,
Somewhere over there
All confined to barracks
was more than I could bear.
I knew you were waiting in the street
I heard your feet,
But could not meet,
My Lily of the Lamplight,
my own Lily Marlene.

Resting in a *billet* [living quarters],
Just behind the line
Even tho' we're parted,
Your lips are close to mine.
You wait where that lantern softly
    gleams,
Your sweet face seems
To haunt my dreams.
My Lily of the Lamplight,
My own Lily Marlene.

German lyrics by Hans Leip
(1915), English lyrics by Tommy
Connor (1942), music by
Norbert Schultze (1938)

▶ A sculpture in Yad Vashem, Israel's memorial
to the Holocaust victims. This work celebrates
Jewish educator and author Janusz Korczak
(1878-1942), shown in this sculpture embracing
children of the orphanage he directed in
Warsaw. He and most of the orphans were
killed in the Treblinka concentration camp.

◀ Lyrics from a song popular during World War II,
"Lily Marlene." It was recorded in German and English
versions and became very popular with both Allied
and German soldiers. The song's popularity suggests
that people fighting in World War II in Europe shared
a sense of separation and loss—no matter which side
they served.

LILY MARLENE, English lyric by Tommie Connor, Music by Norbert
Schultze. Used by permission of Edward B. Marks Music Company.

4

NOW YOU KNOW

- World War II was the most destructive war in history.
- Some 30 to 40 million civilians died in the war.
- Decades later, experts still try to analyze and understand World War II.

Timeline

1919	Treaty of Versailles is signed.
1922	Mussolini becomes prime minister of Italy.
1929	Worldwide economic crisis, the Great Depression, begins.
1933	Hitler becomes chancellor of Germany.
1938	
March	Germany and Austria are united.
September	France, Germany, and the United Kingdom sign the Munich Agreement.
October	Germany begins occupying the Sudetenland, formerly part of Czechoslovakia.
1939	
March	Germany gains control of the remainder of Czechoslovakia.
August	Germany signs an agreement with the Soviet Union.
September 1	Germany invades Poland.
September 3	France and the United Kingdom declare war on Germany.
1940	
April-June	German forces occupy Denmark, Norway, the Netherlands, Belgium, and France.
May 26-June 4	Allied troops are evacuated from Dunkirk in northern France.
June 10	Italy declares war on France and the United Kingdom.
July-September	The Battle of Britain takes place.
September	Beginning of the Blitz, the German bombing campaign against British cities.
1941	
February	German troops sent to support the Italian forces in North Africa.
April 6	Germany invades Yugoslavia and Greece.
June 22	Start of the German invasion of the Soviet Union.
September 8	Siege of Leningrad begins.
December 11	Germany and Italy declare war on the United States.
1942	
August 21	Start of the battle for Stalingrad.
November 8	The Allied invasion of North Africa begins.
1943	
February 2	Last German troops surrender at Stalingrad.
May 13	Italian and German troops surrender in North Africa.
July 4-12	The Battle of Kursk takes place.
July 10	The Allies land on the Italian island of Sicily.
July 24	Allies begin a bombing campaign of Hamburg, Germany; thousands are killed.
September 3	Italy surrenders to the Allies.
September 10	German forces occupy Rome.
1944	
January 22	Allied troops land in Anzio, Italy.
January 27	End of the siege of Leningrad, Russia.
June 4	The Allies enter Rome.
June 6	The Allies land in northern France: D-day.
December 16	A German counterattack begins the Battle of the Bulge.
1945	
March 7	Allied forces first cross the Rhine River into Germany.
April 25	Soviet forces surround Berlin.
April 28	Italian partisans execute Mussolini.
April 30	Hitler commits suicide.
May 7	Germany surrenders to the Allies.
May 8	The Allies declare V-E (Victory in Europe) Day.

Sources

4-5 Document 2 –The Treaty of Versailles. 28 June 1919. *The Avalon Project*. Web. 5 May 2010. Document 4 – Hemingway, Ernest. "Crossing to Germany is Way to Make Money." 1922. Available in *Dateline, Toronto: the Complete Toronto Star Dispatches, 1920-1924*. Ed. William White. New York: Scribner's, 1985. Print.

6-7 Document 2 – Eyewitness to a Nuremberg Rally. 1938. Quoted in Cowles, Virginia. *Looking for Trouble*. New York: Harper, 1941. Print. Document 4 – German schoolteacher. 1940. Quoted in Weber, August, ed. *Uncensored Germany: Letters and News Sent Secretly from Germany to the German Freedom Party*. London: Sidgwick & Jackson, 1940. Print.

8-9 Document 1 – Hitler, Adolph. *Mein Kampf*. 1925-1927. Trans. Ralph Manheim. Boston: Houghton Mifflin, 1943. Print. Document 4 – Anglo-German Declaration. 1938. Quoted in "Anglo-German 'No War' Agreement." *Keesing's Contemporary Archives* 30 Sept. 1938: 3249+. Print. Document 5 – Chamberlain, Neville. Munich agreement speech. 1938. Quoted in Augarde, Tony, ed. *The Oxford Dictionary of Modern Quotations*. New York: Oxford University Press, 1991. Print.

10-11 Document 2 – Hitler, Adolf. *Speeches and Proclamations, 1932-1945*. Vol. 3. Ed. Max Domarus. Wauconda, IL: Bolchazy-Carducci, 1996. Print. Document 3 – Shirer, William. *Berlin Diary: The Journal of a Foreign Correspondent, 1934-1941*. 1941. Baltimore: Johns Hopkins University Press, 2002. Print.

12-13 Document 1 – Rommel, Erwin. *The Rommel Papers*. Ed. B. H. Liddell Hart. 1953. New York: Da Capo Press, 1982. Print. Document 3 – Shirer, William. *Berlin Diary: The Journal of a Foreign Correspondent, 1934-1941*. 1941. Baltimore: Johns Hopkins University Press, 2002. Print.

14-15 Document 2– Klemperer, Victor. *I Will Bear Witness: A Diary of the Nazi Years, 1933-1941*. Trans. Martin Chalmers. New York: Random House, 1998. Print. Document 4 –Beard, John. Interview published in *Their Finest Hour (1941)*. Quoted in "The Battle of Britain, 1940." *EyeWitness to History.com*. Ibis Communications, Inc., 2000. Web. 5 May 2010.

16-17 Document 1 – Bielenberg, Christabel. Description of life in Nazi Germany. Date unknown. Quoted in Smith, Lyn. *Forgotten Voices of the Holocaust*. London: Ebury, 2005. Print. Document 5 – German police order. 1 Sept. 1941. Quoted in Klemperer, Victor. *I Will Bear Witness: A Diary of the Nazi Years, 1933-1941*. New York: Random House, 1998. Print.

18-19 Document 2 – Werner, Herbert A. *Iron Coffins: A Personal Account of the German U-Boat Battles of World War II*. 1969. New York: Da Capo, 2002. Print. Document 4 – Rommel, Erwin. *The Rommel Papers*. Ed. B. H. Liddell Hart. 1953. New York: Da Capo Press, 1982. Print.

20-21 Document 2 – Raus, Erhard. *Panzer Operations: The Eastern Front Memoir of General Raus, 1941-1945*. New York: Da Capo Press, 2005. Print. Document 3 – Klemperer, Victor. *I Will Bear Witness: A Diary of the Nazi Years, 1933-1941*. New York: Random House, 1998. Print.

22-23 Document 2 – Water conservation notice. 1942. Quoted in Longmate, Norman. *How We Lived Then: a History of Everyday Life During the Second World War*. London: Pimlico, 2002. Print. Document 4 – Beevor, Antony. *Stalingrad*. New York: Viking, 1998. Print.

24-25 Document 1 – Gaulle, Charles de. BBC radio broadcast. 18 June 1940. In *The Speeches of General De Gaulle*. Trans. Sheila Mathieu and W. G. Corp. London: Oxford University Press, 1944. Print. Document 3 – Garland, Joseph E. *Unknown Soldiers: Reliving World War II in Europe*. Rockport, Mass.: Protean Press, 2008. Print.

26-27 Document 1 – Jones, Michael. *Leningrad: State of Siege*. New York: Basic Books, 2008. Print.

28-29 Document 1 – Bedard, Allen. Interview published in *The Rock of Anzio (1998)*. Quoted in Whitlock, Flint. *The Rock of Anzio: From Sicily to Dachau, a History of the 45th Infantry*. Boulder, Colo.: Westview Press, 1998. Print. Document 4 – Yugoslav father's letter to child. 1941. In "Such Is Your Heritage." *Time* 25 Jan. 1943: 33. Print.

30-31 Document 2 – Stalin, Joseph. Order No. 227. 28 July 1942. Quoted in Beevor, Antony. *Stalingrad*. New York: Viking, 1998. Print.

Document 4 – General Karl Strecker. Quoted in Beevor, Antony. *Stalingrad*. New York: Viking, 1998. Print.

32-33 Document 2 – Greenman, Leon. Interview by Lyn Smith. Date unknown. Quoted in Smith, Lyn. *Forgotten Voices of the Holocaust*. London: Ebury, 2005. Print. Document 3 – Katzenelson, Yitzhak. *The Song of the Murdered Jewish People*. Quoted in Gilbert, Martin. *The Holocaust: A History of the Jews of Europe During the Second World War*. New York: H. Holt, 1985. Print.

34-35 Document 1 – German soldier. Description of Stalingrad battle in 1942. Quoted in Beevor, Antony. *Stalingrad*. New York: Viking, 1998. Print. Document 3 – Raus, Erhard. *Panzer Operations: The Eastern Front Memoir of General Raus, 1941-1945*. New York: Da Capo Press, 2005.

36-37 Document 1 – Captain James T. Compton. Court martial proceedings. 1943. Quoted in Weingartner, James J. "Massacre at Biscari: Patton and an American War Crime." *Historian* 52.1(1989): 24-39. Print.

Document 3 – Soldier in the Anzio trenches in 1944. Quoted in Atkinson, Rick. *The Day of Battle: The War in Sicily and Italy, 1943–44*. New York: Henry Holt, 2007. Print.

38-39 Document 1 – German leaflet. 1945. Quoted in Daugherty, William E. *A Psychological Warfare Casebook*. Baltimore: Johns Hopkins Press, 1958. Print. Document 3 –Schirach, Baldur von. "Unsere Fahne flattert uns voran." 1934. Quoted in Bosmajian, Hamida. *Sparing the Child*. New York: Routledge, 2002. Print.

40-41 Document 2 – *Casablanca*. Dir. Michael Curtiz. Warner Bros., 1942. Film. Document 3 – *The Longest Day*. Dir. Ken Annakin. 20th Century Fox, 1962. Film.

42-43 Document 2 – Khrushchev, Nikita. *Memoirs of Nikita Khrushchev. Volume I, Commissar, 1918–1945*. Pennsylvania State University, 2004. Print. Document 4 – Hobart, Percy. On the value of tanks. Quoted in Constable, Trevor. "The Little-Known Story of Percy Hobart." *Journal for Historical Review* 18.1 (1999): 2. Print.

44-45 Document 1 – German Soldier. Letter to his wife. 1943. Quoted in Evans, Richard J. *The Third Reich at War*. New York: Penguin Press, 2009. Print. Document 3 – Liebeskind, Helmut. Interview. Date unknown. Quoted in Miller, Russell. *Nothing Less Than Victory: The Oral History of D-Day*. London: Pimlico, 2000. Print.

46-47 Document 2 – Eisenhower, Dwight D. "Eisenhower's Crusade in Europe." *Time* 13 Dec. 1948" 130+. Print. Document 3 – Captain Joseph T. Dawson. 1944. Quoted in Lewis, John E. *D-Day as They Saw It*. New York: Carroll & Graf, 2004. Print.

48-49 Document 2 – French resistance fighter. Quoted in Rohrlich, Ruby. *Resisting the Holocaust*. New York: Berg, 1998. Print.York: Berg, 1998. Print. Document 3 – Kovner, Abba. Speech to fellow resistance fighters. 1 Jan. 1942. Quoted in Rohrlich, Ruby. *Resisting the Holocaust*. New York: Berg, 1998. Print.

50-51 Document 2 – Koch, Traute. Description of the Hamburg bombing in 1943. Quoted in Middlebrook, Martin. *The Battle of Hamburg: Allied Bomber Forces Against a German City in 1943*. London: Allen Lane, 1980. Document 4 – Harris, Arthur. Letter to Norman Bottomley. 29 Mar. 1945. Quoted in Saward, Dudley. *Bomber Harris: The Story of Marshal of the Royal Air Force, Sir Arthur Harris*. Garden City, N.Y.: Doubleday, 1985. Print.

52-53 Document 2 – Walb, Lore. Diary. Mar. 1945. Quoted in Evans, Richard J. *The Third Reich at War*. New York: Penguin Press, 2009. Print. Document 3 – Foley, John. *Mailed Fist*. London: Panther, 1957. Print.

54-55 Documents 2 and 3 – German women. Quoted in Smith, Lyn. *Forgotten Voices of the Holocaust*. London: Ebury, 2005. Print.

56-57 Document 1 – Panter-Downes, Mollie. "Letter from London." *The New Yorker* 19 May 1945: 44+. Document 3 – Moorehead, Alan. *Eclipse*. 1945. New York: Harper & Row, 1968. Print.

58-59 Document 2 – Raboud, Jacques. Quoted in Terkel, Studs. *The Good War*. Pantheon. 1984. Print. Document 3 – Connor, Tommie. "Lily Marlene." 1944. Quoted in Edward. B. Marks Music Corporation. Advertisement. *Billboard* 16 Sept. 1944: 13. Print.

Additional resources

Books

Angels of Mercy: The Army Nurses of World War II, by Betsy Kuhn, Atheneum, 1999

Children in the Holocaust and World War II: Their Secret Diaries, by Laurel Holliday, Washington Square Press, 1995

The Good Fight: How World War II Was Won, by Stephen E. Ambrose, Atheneum, 2001

I Have Lived a Thousand Years: Growing Up in the Holocaust, by Livia Bitton-Jackson, Simon & Schuster Books for Young Readers, 1997

Living in Nazi Germany (Exploring Cultural History series), by Elaine Halleck, Greenhaven Press, 2004

World War II (Opposing Viewpoints in World History series), by Don Nardo, Walker, 1992

World War II: Northwest Europe, 1944-1945 (World War II: Essential Histories), by Russell and Stephen Hart, Rosen Publishing Group, 2010

Ultra Hush-Hush: Espionage and Special Missions (Outwitting the Enemy: Stories from the Second World War series), by Stephen Shapiro and Tina Forrester, Annick Press, 2003

Websites

http://www.bbc.co.uk/history/worldwars/wwtwo/
The British Broadcasting Company (BBC) created this interactive site on World War II.

http://www.nationalarchives.gov.uk/education/homefront/preparations/default.htm
A site by the National Archives of the United Kingdom explores World War II in Europe and its effect on civilians.

http://www.nationalarchives.gov.uk/education/lessons/lesson30.htm
A site by the National Archives of the United Kingdom helps young adults use primary documents to explore the choices made by the British government in the 1930's, in the days leading up to World War II.

http://digitalcollections.smu.edu/all/cul/hgp/
A collection of historic documents published by the U.S. government during World War II.

Index

Index

Acknowledgments

AKG-Images: 10 (Ullstein Bild), 11, 13 (Ullstein Bild), 15 (Ullstein Bild), 16, 23, 27, 32, 53, 55 (Ullstein Bild); **A.P. Photos:** 26; **Art Archive:** 1, 18, 19, 20, 30, 34, 35, 40, 44, 46, 47 (National Archives, Washington D.C.); **Corbis:** 6 (Bettmann), 7, 8, 12, 22, 28 (Bettmann), 36, 38 (Bettmann), 45 (Hulton-Deutsch Collection), 48, 50 (Bettmann), 54 (Michael St. Maur Sheil), 56, 57 (Yevgeny Khaldei), 58 (Bettmann); **Getty:** 29 (Popperfoto), 37 (FPG/Hulton Archive), 43; **Library of Congress:** 25; **Shutterstock:** 17 right (riekephotos), 31 (Alfredo Ragazzoni), 59 (Corky Buczyk); **Topfoto:** 4, 5, 9, 14, 17 left, 24, 39, 42, 51, 52.

Cover main image: **Corbis** (Richard Klune); inset image: **Art Archive** (National Archives, Washington D.C.)